SNAP HAPPY

SNAP HAPPY

DIGITAL AND FILM CAMERA SKILLS FOR KIDS

PETER COPE

CARLTON
BOOKS

THIS IS A CARLTON BOOK

Text and design copyright © Carlton Books Limited 2005

This edition published by
Carlton Books Limited 2005
20 Mortimer Street
London W1T 3JW

A CIP catalogue record for this book is available from
the British Library.

ISBN 1 84442 409 X

Printed and bound in Dubai

Executive Editor: Lisa Dyer
Art Editor: Emma Wicks
Design: Ben Ruocco
Copy Editor: Lara Maiklem
Picture Researcher: Sarah Edwards
Production: Caroline Alberti

CONTENTS

INTRODUCTION

Throughout history, human beings have invented various devices to help them capture images. Some of the great painters of Renaissance Europe used optical devices called 'camera obscurae' to project images on to canvases to make sure that the proportions of their drawings were correct. At the turn of the nineteenth century Thomas Wedgwood, the famous English potter, created silhouette 'sun pictures' using a basic photographic chemical mix that was later to form the basis of photo printing.

Photography, as we know it today, began to appear from the mid-nineteenth century. From around this time, photo studios were set up in almost every town and even the poorest people would save hard to have family portraits taken. People thought photographers were like magicians – they worked with strange chemicals and their photographs were created in total darkness.

In the early twentieth century photography took on a less romantic role as it became increasingly important in reporting news events. Wars and events occurring on the other side of the world could now be shown in graphic detail to those who would otherwise never get the chance to see them.

ABOVE Throughout the nineteenth century, photographic portraits were considered in the same way as original paintings – valued artworks that took pride of place in the home.

The early years of the twentieth century were also notable for another photography first – the launch of the Kodak Brownie in the USA. Retailing for just $1, it was a cheap, basic, no-nonsense camera that made photography available to everyone. For half a century the Box Brownie camera helped ordinary people record their lives. You can still find old examples of this classic camera in garage sales and Internet auction sites.

ABOVE Kodak ran with the slogan 'Any Schoolboy or Girl Can Make Good Pictures with the Brownie Camera'. The company knew what children wanted for Christmas in the 1900s.

TIMELINE

- **1500s:** The camera obscura was used by artists to project images on to canvases.
- **1727:** First photosensitive chemicals are produced.
- **1800:** Thomas Wedgwood produces sun pictures by placing opaque objects on chemically treated paper and leather.
- **1826:** French pioneer Nicéphore Niépce produces the first permanent print (one that does not deteriorate in light).
- **1834:** Henry Fox Talbot produces the first negative images that can be used to create positive prints.
- **1837:** Louis Daguerre produces images on silver-plated copper, coated with silver iodide. The 'Daguerrotype' would be popular for decades.
- **1853:** Antoine Claudet patents the stereoscope, based on work by Jules Duboscq, and stereoscopic, or 3D, photography begins. Photographers could now take photos that appeared in three dimensions, creating the depth viewed in the original scene.
- **1861:** Colour photography is demonstrated by Scottish physicist James Clerk-Maxwell, who projects a colour image of a tartan ribbon.

These days, photography has never been more popular or easy, particularly with the introduction of digital technology. Cameras were once limited to film, and the shape and size was dictated by the need for a lens that was large enough to cast an image on the film. Different film types were developed and introduced over the years, aiming to create cameras that were more convenient to use and carry. But once digital camera advances removed the need for films, a whole new generation of cameras were born.

Today's cameras have been developed from the Brownie, but they offer incredible performance and many additional features. George Eastman, the man responsible for inventing the Brownie, would have been very impressed by the technology that is available to us today. Cameras are now even simpler to use than his models and yet offer better results. He would probably have also been amazed by the way cameras are finding their way into other devices and gadgets – camera phones, PDA phones, movie cameras that take photos, still cameras that take movies, cameras that play digital music, the list just keeps growing. And the new developments don't stop there. We no longer need to despatch our films to a lab and wait eagerly for their return. We can now get immediate results and, thanks to computers, if the photographs don't look right, we can make them better or even create scenes and collages that could never exist in the real world!

In this book we'll explore photography today. We'll take a look at the incredible range of both film and digital cameras and the features that they offer us, and show you how to take great photos that you'll be proud to share and display.

- 1880: George Eastman founds the Eastman Dry Plate Company in Rochester, New York, which later becomes Kodak.
- 1900: Kodak Brownie box camera is launched.
- 1907: Colour film arrives on the market.
- 1924: The Leica – the first commercially available, high-quality 35mm camera – is launched.
- 1963: Polaroid produces the first ever colour instant film.
- 1972: Kodak introduces 110-format cameras to deliver pocketable simple-to-use photography to a new generation.
- 1982: Sony demonstrates the Mavica 'still video' camera; this was the first commercial 'digital' camera with images recorded on to a mini disc.
- 1983: Kodak launches the ultra-compact disc camera system.
- 1990s: Digital cameras appear for the home-computer market.
- 1992: Kodak introduces PhotoCD: digital images produced from conventional photos.
- 2000s: Digital cameras become widespread and outsell conventional cameras. Cameras appear in other devices, including phones and PDAs.

GETTING TO KNOW YOUR CAMERA

To many of us, the camera is a mysterious black box. We point the front of the box at the object we have chosen to take a picture of and, as if by magic, the scene is captured. Although you don't need to know all the difficult technical details, getting acquainted with the key controls and recognizing the main features on your camera will help you to take a better picture.

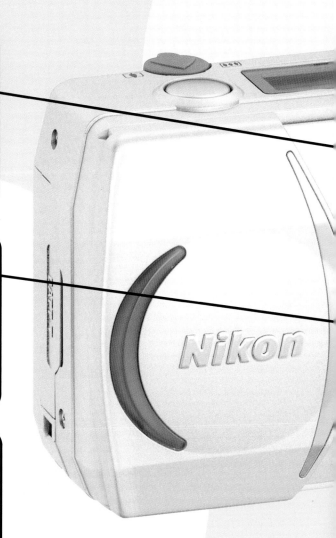

Viewfinder
The viewfinder gives you a miniature preview of how your picture is going to turn out. By looking through the viewfinder you can check that your subject is correctly positioned and composed (we will look more closely at composition later). If your camera has a zoom lens, the viewfinder adjusts as you zoom in and out so that you can see how close or far away you are from your subject.

Camera Lens
The lens focuses the light rays that come off the subject on to film in a conventional camera, or the CCD (Charge Coupled Device) sensor in a digital camera. Some lenses are fixed – this means that they always reproduce images to the same scale. Others are zoom lenses that enable us to take close-up pictures of more distant objects.

Film
Conventional cameras capture the image on films, which need to be removed from the camera when they are full and developed. There are lots of different types of film. Digital cameras use a light sensitive electronic sensor (a CCD) instead of film.

LEFT The viewfinder is essential to composing photos. Indicators, like the coloured lights shown here, let you know when the camera is in focus and when the exposure is correct.

LEFT Many people now have digital cameras, but conventional types of film in colour and black and white are still available.

Flash
When you take a photo at night or in dark conditions the result can be blurred or discoloured. The additional light from a built-in flash, as shown here, can let you take good photos in situations where there is not enough light. On some cameras you can create even more light by using a bigger and more powerful flashgun.

Shutter
Buried within the camera, between the lens and the film (or sensor in digital cameras), the shutter determines how long the film or sensor is exposed to light. In many cameras, the camera, usually in combination with the aperture, automatically calculates the amount of time that the shutter is open for, normally less than $\frac{1}{100}$ second.

THE DIGITAL CAMERA
The back of a digital camera is dominated by an LCD (Liquid Crystal Display) panel, like a mini television screen, that guides you while you are taking the photo and lets you check the results afterwards. On many models some controls and buttons are arranged around the screen. The key difference between a conventional camera and a digital one is that digital cameras have no film. Instead, they have an electronic, light-sensitive chip that records the image on a memory card.

LEFT You can play back your images by viewing them through the LCD screen and delete any that you don't want.

Aperture
The aperture iris controls the amount of light that is allowed into the camera. Large apertures let in more light and small apertures less light. Varying the iris ensures that, as light levels change between bright daylight and perhaps twilight, the optimum amount of light enters the camera in order to take the best shots.

CHOOSING YOUR IDEAL CAMERA

Cameras come in all shapes and sizes and digital technology has made it possible to produce cameras in a far wider selection. Digital cameras are even incorporated into other devices, such as phones or handheld computers. Here is a selection of different sorts of cameras.

Disposable Cameras

Disposable cameras (sometimes called single-use) are conventional cameras that come preloaded with film. Once you have used up the film, you take the whole camera to a photo store and get back just the prints and negatives. This camera is cheap to buy but you cannot reload it with a new roll of film and reuse it.

These cameras don't take the best quality of pictures, but they are a great solution if you forget to take your camera with you on a day out, or if you do not want to risk damaging your regular camera.

Despite being 'disposable', these cameras are fairly environmentally friendly in that, once the photo store has removed your film, virtually all of the camera is recycled.

ABOVE Disposable cameras are rather basic, but some have a flash and others are available in a waterproof housing – ideal for photos on the beach or even underwater!

LEFT Fuji's pendant-like Q1 model comes in different colours and even multicoloured floral designs. This model is available as a digital camera and a conventional, film-based one, too.

Camera Phones

Do you carry a mobile phone around with you everywhere? Would you like to have a camera with you, too? Then why not get a camera phone? Many of the more recent designs now rival the photo quality of simple digital cameras and can even record movie clips.

You can also use camera phones to share your photos instantly with your friends. Send the pictures from your phone to a photo lab and get prints that will be delivered to your door in just a couple of days.

Fashion Cameras

Who said that cameras have to be a rectangular black box? Cameras today can be fashion accessories too! These colourful, curvaceous designs not only look great, but they also take excellent photos. Fashion cameras can be either conventional or digital and come in a range of shapes, sizes, colours and prices.

RIGHT A camera phone is ideal for taking with you everywhere. Although photo quality may not be as good as some cameras, it makes up for this in its portability.

ABOVE The Olympus m[mju:] range of cameras has been popular for many years. The m[mju:] mini is a digital model that comes in a range of colours so you can choose one to match your mood or your favourite colour!

Compact Cameras

This is the largest selling type of camera – both film-based and digital. It is small enough to carry in a bag, or even a large pocket, and it is easy to use, offering excellent performance and lots of features.

Most compact cameras are fully automatic – once you've turned it on, all the settings are adjusted automatically by the camera to ensure that you get a great shot every time. If conditions are difficult – if it's dark or hard for the camera to focus – a light or bleep will alert you to the problem, which allows you to turn on the flash or give your camera some support to prevent blurring.

More sophisticated compact cameras also include some semi-automatic modes. These cameras adjust some of their settings automatically and some can be done manually. This gives the best results for, for example, action and sports photography, portraits or even night-time photography.

ABOVE Compact cameras can be simple or sophisticated. The Canon IXUS camera has fully automatic no-frills controls, delivered in a streamlined, minimalist casing.

LEFT Special plastic housing for compact cameras lets you operate all the camera controls, even when it's wet, dusty or underwater when you're swimming.

UNDERWATER CAMERAS

Do you spend a lot of time at the beach or in the pool, or do you just like getting wet? If so, underwater cameras could be your perfect match. And they're not just useful in water. The watertight cases of these cameras also make them ideal for use in dusty, muddy or sandy conditions.

Special underwater cameras may be very expensive, but you can buy waterproof housings for some ordinary compact cameras that give you both a useful day-to-day camera and a waterproof version for the beach. Cheaper still are waterproof disposable cameras, ideal to pack for holidays or action weekends away.

RIGHT For occasional wet use, disposable, single-use waterproof cameras are a good choice.

Serious Cameras

If you plan to take your photography seriously, you might find that all the cameras we've looked at so far don't give you quite enough features. You may, for example, want to photograph very small objects, like bugs or flowers, or you might want to use lenses that let you take photos of very small distant objects, such as birds or wildlife. The automatic and semi-automatic cameras that we have covered so far are extremely limited when it comes to this type of specialist photography.

At such events as a sports game, professional photographers will use SLR (Single Lens Reflex) cameras. You can change the lens – perhaps for one that focuses very close, or for a lens that acts like a telescope – and you can add other accessories, such as powerful flashguns or coloured, special-effect lens filters. With an SLR there is almost nothing you can't photograph. The drawback? They take a while to learn to use properly and they can be really expensive!

BELOW RIGHT Some SLR cameras don't have interchangeable lenses, but still offer a tremendous range of features – they also cost much less. In this cutaway picture you can see all the internal chambers that make up the camera.

BELOW Some photography needs special equipment to do the job properly. This panoramic camera takes a picture over more than one film frame, giving an elongated image.

WILD AND WACKY

Many people take their photography very seriously, but for most of us taking photos is about having fun. Here is a small selection of more unusual cameras that will help make recording all those memorable events even more fun.

Instant Cameras

Before digital cameras made it possible to see photos moments after they were shot, instant cameras, or Polaroid cameras (until recently Polaroid was the exclusive manufacturer of instant cameras) as they were known, were the thing to have. In fact, there is still something magical about taking a photo and sharing the print moments later.

These days, Polaroid and Fujifilm make a wide range of instant cameras, producing conventional, credit card- and thumbnail-sized prints. When you and your friends have finished giggling over them, stick your instant pictures in a scrapbook, illustrated diaries or store them in your wallet as keepsakes.

LEFT AND RIGHT Instant cameras are the only way to get prints on the spot.

Three-Dimensional Cameras

The Victorians had a huge appetite for photography and three-dimensional (or 3D, stereo) was popular. This medium allowed people to see photographs as they appeared in real life, with true depth. The photographs were clever, but also difficult to view as they required special apparatus. For this reason 3D photos quickly fell out of fashion.

Other methods of producing 3D photographs have come and gone over the years and today it is possible to buy cameras that take photographs that make you just want to reach out and touch them. If you would like to give try it, 3D cameras can be found on the Internet and in some photo stores. You can also buy viewers that help you to get real depth in your photos.

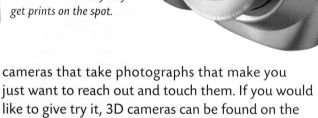

LEFT This Loreo 3D camera takes two photos simultaneously. With the special viewer, included with the camera kit, you can see the world in three dimensions.

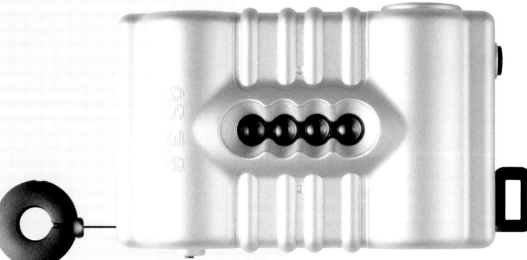

ABOVE The Supersampler has four lenses for shooting four consecutive photos.

Lomography

The Lomo Camera Company in the old Soviet Union (now Russia) used to produce serious cameras for sale in the Soviet Union. Now Lomo markets a wide range of cameras around the world – some are sensible, and others are definitely not! The Colorsplash, for example, uses a powerful flashgun with coloured lenses to produce some crazy false colour effects. Supersamplers take multiple shots on a single frame of film, just a split second apart.

Lomo now has a huge cult following, with those who enjoy the cameras calling themselves 'Lomographers'. If you like experimenting with photography, Lomo cameras, which are modestly priced, are a good place to start.

RIGHT Here's the four-frame in-motion result from a Supersampler. Caught in the act!

CAMERA CONTROLS: WHAT THEY DO AND WHY YOU NEED THEM

Successful photography depends on knowing what your camera can and can't do. Although most cameras today are fully automatic, understanding how the controls work will ensure you get terrific results every time.

ABOVE Sharp focus is crucial. Even a slightly blurred shot, like the one on the right, looks terrible, so take a moment to ensure your subject is focused correctly.

Focusing

It is essential to achieve sharp focusing in a photo as poor focusing can ruin your shots. Fortunately, most of today's cameras have accurate autofocusing mechanisms which ensure that, when you press the shutter release button to take a photo, the camera lens will focus on your subject.

In most cameras, when you press and hold the shutter release only halfway, the camera focuses and then the focus locks. You can then adjust the camera's view (to put the subject off-centre, for example), sure in the knowledge that the main subject will still be in sharp focus.

Exposure

Cameras are rather like our own eyes. Give them too much light and they are dazzled; too little light and they struggle to make out what's lurking in the gloom. In photography we call too much light 'overexposure'. Overexposed photos are too bright and much of the composition is featureless and white. Too little light is known as 'underexposure'. An underexposed photo lacks colour and has muddy, dark, shadowed areas.

Fortunately, the controls in automatic cameras are good at detecting the amount of light and adjusting the camera so that the right quantity of light hits the film or electronic sensor. It does this by varying the exposure time (the length of time that the shutter in the camera opens to let light in) or the aperture of the lens – the aperture is the width of the opening of the lens, the wider the opening, the more light that can get in.

ABOVE In the picture on the right, the depth of field was decreased by increasing the aperture. This makes the subject stand out.

LEFT to RIGHT

Too little light results in underexposure in the photo on the far left. The photo in the centre was taken with the correct exposure, but the photo on the right was taken with too much light, meaning it is overexposed.

DEPTH OF FIELD

You might be wondering why we have two exposure controls – aperture and exposure time? Surely we could use a constant exposure time and just vary the aperture, or use a fixed aperture and change the exposure time. The fact is that having a combination of controls allows us to get more creative results.

For example, if you were taking a picture of a galloping horse, you could force the camera to use a large aperture, which would mean you could use a short exposure time to 'freeze' the fast action. Also, by varying the aperture, we can alter the depth of field – the amount of the photo that is in sharp focus. With a small aperture, close objects and distant ones will be in focus. The wider the aperture, the smaller the amount of the scene that will be in focus. This method is ideal for portraits as it really makes your subject stand out.

UNDERSTANDING LENSES

It is the camera's lens that creates an image, which in turn is recorded (either on film or electronic sensor) as a photograph. In some cameras the lens can be a very simple one. It won't adjust to focus for objects at different distances, nor can you zoom it, to make objects appear closer or further away. These are called fixed or 'focus free' lenses. You will find them fine for taking portrait-type photos, but when you try to take other shots, such as close-ups or distant views, the results can be disappointing.

ABOVE This photo was taken with a camera set to a normal focal length. It is roughly what we would see with our eyes.

ABOVE By zooming out, we can see much more of the surroundings, but the subject is smaller.

Zoom Lenses

Most cameras today offer autofocusing. In all but the most basic cameras you will be able to adjust the focal length of the lens, too – like changing the magnification of a telescope or microscope. We call a lens like this a zoom lens.

When we 'zoom out' we make the focal length shorter and we can get a wider view through the lens – this is sometimes also called a wide-angle view. When we lengthen the focal length, which is done by changing the position of individual lenses within the zoom lens itself, we can 'zoom in' on a small portion of a scene, such as one person in a crowd. The greater the focal length, the smaller the area we can zoom in on. This is sometimes called a telephoto lens.

Viewfinder

When we change the focal length, we need to see how this adjustment is changing the scene that appears in our photos. In digital cameras this is easy because the scene is shown in the LCD display on the back. Many other cameras have a zoom viewfinder, so when you zoom the lens, the viewfinder will adjust its view, too.

LEFT Zooming in with the lens lets you fill the photo with a small part of the scene – in this case the girl becomes the clear subject of the photo and the colourful surroundings have more impact.

ZOOMING TIPS
- Zoom out when you want to take a photo in a small space or indoors.
- Try using the wide-angle zoom setting to take some weird portraits: photograph your subject close up!
- For more impact, adjust the zoom range to fill the frame with your chosen subject.
- You can buy adaptor lenses for your compact camera to give even wider wide-angle views, or more magnified telephoto shots.

ABOVE To get a shot like this, adjust the zoom while you're taking it.

Colour Balance

You will only find this setting on digital cameras. The camera uses colour balance to recognize the kind of lighting that the photographs are being taken in. You can choose between daylight, cloudy, artificial (tungsten bulbs) and fluorescent lighting settings. If you set the colour balance incorrectly, you could get some strange colour casts. Fortunately, most cameras have an auto setting that automatically sets the right colour balance for the scene.

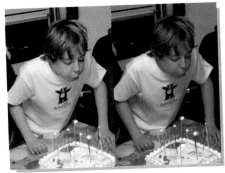

FAR LEFT This photo was taken with the correct colour balance.

LEFT The same scene with the colour balance set to artificial lighting.

ABOVE An indoor shot with the colour balance set to artificial, see left, and daylight, see right.

ACCESSORIES

Take a look in any camera store and you will see shelves full of 'essential' accessories – but are they really so necessary? We've sifted through all these extras and add-ons to bring you a rated guide of the good, the bad and the ugly.

Essential

Film/Memory Cards: If you've got a conventional camera, you'll need to feed it film. There is plenty on offer and it can be rather confusing, but if you are after an all-round print film, look for mid-range sensitivity (ISO 200). ISO is a measure of a film's sensitivity to light. ISO 400 film is twice as sensitive as ISO 200 and requires an exposure only half as long. This type of film tends to be the most popular and keenly priced, so look out for good-value multipacks.

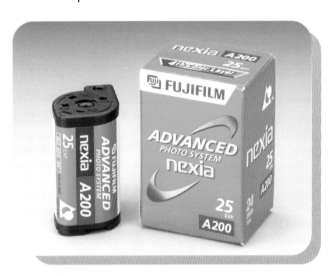

If you've got a digital camera you will need memory cards to store the images on. Annoyingly, most digital cameras, even high-performance ones, only come with a single, small-capacity memory card, which means that you can't shoot too many pictures before having to download the images on to your computer. Arm yourself with some high capacity cards; they don't cost too much and it means that you can shoot for ages before downloading to a computer.

Batteries: Whatever type of camera you have, except a disposable one, you will need batteries to keep it running. Always make sure you have an extra set, or two, as there's nothing more frustrating than running out of power just as you are about to capture that award-winning shot!

Highly Recommended

Cases: Storage cases don't just keep your camera in good condition, preventing damage from knocks and bumps, but they also protect the camera from dust, sand and rain.

Rechargeable Batteries: If you take many pictures, particularly on digital, you will find yourself using lots of batteries and this can get expensive. Rechargeable batteries are more expensive per unit, but will pay for themselves in the long term. Don't forget the charger!

Card Reader: One for the digital camera user. Card readers may be permanently connected to your camera to allow your memory cards to be quickly downloaded. This is faster than connecting the camera directly to a computer and it saves on precious batteries, too.

Useful

Straps: Carrying your camera around all day can be tiring and you run the risk of dropping it, so consider investing in a shoulder or wrist strap, if one wasn't included with your camera when you bought it. These have the added benefit of freeing your hands for changing film, memory cards or batteries.

External Flash: Only some cameras have the facilities to connect one of these, but an external flash gives you the opportunity to produce more comprehensive effects.

Filters: Filters for conventional cameras serve the same purpose as white balance on a digital camera by ensuring that your photos are colour corrected. You can also use coloured filters for more extreme colour effects. Digital camera users may want to give coloured filters a miss as the same effects can be done later with your computer software.

BELOW Colour correction filters help ensure that film and lighting conditions are perfectly matched. They can also be used to allow Indoor film to be used outdoors and vice versa.

Tripods and Supports: To avoid vibration and shake in your photos, you'll need a firm support. A small beanbag makes a great impromptu support but, to position the camera at all angles, a tripod is best. If you plan to take lots of night-time photos then consider a tripod as essential, rather than just useful, since this type of photography needs a longer shutter speed and can blur. A monopod is a more compact, one-legged alternative.

Don't Bother

Effects Filters: These give colour and pattern effects, but you will soon tire of them and they are expensive.

Small Capacity Memory Cards: The fact that digital camera manufacturers pack a paltry 16MB memory card with their cameras is more due to economics than good sense. You may find these on sale very cheaply, but larger capacities (256MB and more) are now comparatively cheap. These will let you shoot lots more photos before filling up.

Lens Cleaning Kits: Unpleasant chemicals can be found in some kits that will cause more harm than good. The best way to have a pristine lens is to avoid smudges in the first place. Failing that, a simple lint-free cloth and blower brush are safer — and cheaper.

Bargain Batteries: At best these will be poor performers, at worst they can split and leak chemicals into your precious camera. Some have even been known to catch fire. Stick with reputable names, either following the manufacturers' recommendations or selecting from a camera store.

TAKING PHOTOS

Playing with cameras is fun, even more so if they are part of a multifunctional device, such as a phone. Modern technology has made it possible to take photographs simply by pressing one button so there really is no reason for a photo to be technically bad. However, technically perfect photos aren't always good photos. To take a really good photo we need to learn some clever techniques and just a few rules.

HOW TO TAKE GREAT PHOTOS

Good Composition

The way in which you place subjects and objects in your photo is vital. Most people naturally place the most important part of the scene in the centre of the picture, but this does not always result in a good photo. Putting an object in the centre means that there is often quite a bit of empty space either side and above it, particularly in the case of a portrait.

It's much better to position your subject dead centre, focus the camera on it and then move the subject to one side, up a little, or even both. There is an easy rule for creating powerful compositions called the 'Rule of Thirds' (see below). Use this and you will rarely go wrong!

Another useful compositional idea is to make sure that any moving subjects are moving towards the centre of the photo. If you're photographing some people walking, make sure they are walking into the photo and towards the centre. You'll get the same result with cars, horses or anything mobile.

THE RULE OF THIRDS

To use the Rule of Thirds you need to imagine that your viewfinder, or LCD screen, has three horizontal and three vertical lines running across it, dividing the area into nine squares. Some digital cameras make this easy by providing an overlaid grid at the touch of a button. Use these grid lines (imaginary or real) to place subjects in your scene.

Place the horizon along one of the two horizontal lines. Then, put the key elements of your composition, such as a friend's face, at the point where two lines cross. If you have two important subjects and you can manage to get each of them on a crossing point, you will create a really powerful composition for your photo!

LEFT The automatic grid feature on some digital cameras makes using the Rule of Thirds simple – just place important features at the cross points.

Experiment With Angles

The most obvious way to take a photo is to put it to your eye and shoot. In photo terms, this means that most of your photos will be taken from the same height, with the result that we see everything from the same position. You can achieve more interesting results by using your camera in different positions; for example, by lying down and looking upward or by holding the camera over your head and pointing downward. You could even try taking pictures at an angle.

If you are photographing people, shooting from below makes them look more important and from above, more timid. This is a great way to get character into your photos. If you are photographing tall buildings, rotating the camera diagonally allows you to get the entire building in the shot, and also gives an added impression of height.

Get in Close

It is very easy to take pictures with a lot of wasted space around a subject. This is particularly true if you shoot subjects from a distance. Often you don't realize that your subject doesn't actually take up much of the photo until it's too late. So always think about filling your frame. Either move in closer to the subject or use the camera's zoom lens. A frame filled with the subject is always more impressive!

Frame Your Shots

Whether you enjoy taking landscape photos or portraits, you'll get better results if you frame your subjects properly. We're not talking about wooden frames that you buy from the local art store; we mean scenery that can be used as a prop to give your photos some depth. Suitable frames might be a doorway, arch or leaves and trees, through which you can shoot your subject.

Get the Light Right

The light sensitivity of cameras and films today is such that we can take photos across a wide range of conditions, both very light and very dark. However, even in the brightest light – or perhaps we should say especially in the brightest of light – you can get disappointing results because of shadows and shading. Because cameras are so good at getting the light levels right, often they don't register when a little extra light is needed to counteract shadows. For these conditions you can use the 'backlight control' on the camera.

This control is normally used to get the light levels right when the sun is behind your subjects, but it can also work well in lighting up photos that might otherwise have too much shadow. This control works especially well with snow photos, ensuring the snow is bright white and not left looking rather muddy.

ABOVE The image on the left is shot without backlight control, with the result that the person is placed in shadow. On the right backlight control is used.

Keep Attention on Your Subject

Whatever your photographic interest, your photos need a subject – this can be a friend, a building, a special keepsake, your dog, the list goes on. It is important to ensure that your subject is clearly visible. You might think that getting the focus right and the picture well composed is all you need to do, but sometimes it's not enough. Take care when placing your subject against a cluttered background or near other people or objects. Make it very obvious who or what is the centre of attention.

BREAKING THE RULES

We have mentioned lots of rules on these pages, but don't feel you have to follow all of them every time. They are rules that are designed to help, rather than dictate, your photography. In fact, some very good and unusual photography comes from breaking the established rules.

- Don't use the Rule of Thirds for every landscape shot.
- Don't get in close if, perhaps, you want to show how small a subject is in the wider landscape.
- Use a cluttered background if you feel it adds to the photo.
- Don't use unusual angles if the resulting photo looks just plain weird!

Getting Close

Insects, flowers and even jewellery all make really great photo subjects, but you'll need to get up close. It's only when you're close that you see all of the intricate detail.

Most cameras have a minimum focusing distance, which lets you get pretty close to your subject, and many cameras now have a macro mode, too. In macro you can create an image on your film, or CCD sensor, that is approximately life size – when this type of image is printed, the results can be remarkable. Digital cameras are more effective in macro mode for two main reasons. First, you can use the LCD panel to ensure that the subject is in sharp focus – focus is critical at close range. Second, the digital cameras have a better type of lens for close focusing.

If you've got a conventional camera, don't be put off taking close-ups; you just need to be a bit more careful with your distances. Also, by making sure that you shoot in the brightest possible conditions you can get much better depth of field.

ABOVE Flowers are perfect subjects for using a macro feature.

Use Your Flash – Carefully

Using the camera's flashgun means that you can get some impressive shots even when the natural light is poor. You can also use the light from a flashgun to help prevent dark shadows in bright daylight. Some cameras have a flash setting called 'Fill-in'. This gives a small burst of flashlight that is suitable for brightening shadows, but without being too obvious. It's also important to realize how powerful your flash is. Photographs taken at night using a flash can often be disappointing because the subjects are beyond the range at which the flash can successfully light a scene. You can find details of how far your flash will reach in the camera manual, but a good guide for most on-camera flashguns is to ensure that your subjects are never more than about 3 metres (10 feet) away.

ABOVE Keep within the flash range of the camera and you can get some really fun night shots.

Take Vertical Photos

Cameras can take vertical photos as well as horizontal, so why do we shoot almost all our photos horizontally? Turning your camera through 90 degrees will give you some great compositions and adds interest and variety to your photo collection. It's also almost essential for close-up photos of people or landmarks!

GETTING REALLY CLOSE

If you want to get even closer than the macro mode permits, or your camera doesn't have a macro mode, don't be discouraged. Camera stores usually stock close-up lenses for most cameras, which can be fitted over the camera lens to let you get even closer. You can also buy adaptors that will allow your camera to link to a microscope for microscopic photography.

One word of warning: with macro settings and macro lenses it is easy to get so close to your subject that the camera lens causes shadows. Pay particular attention to the lighting.

OOPS!

Our photos can develop brilliantly, but they can also go horribly wrong. We've all taken a shot that we think will turn out amazing, only to be badly disappointed with the result when it's been printed. It's so easy only to pay attention to the subject of the photo and not to notice what is going on around, behind or even in front of it. When we get the print back, suddenly our error is there for all to see. Here's just a classic few photo howlers that even professionals produce now and again!

The Tree in the Head

Surrealist artists worked long and hard to create paintings that featured odd compositions, such as a person with a tree sprouting from their head. If you line your subject up with a distant tree, flag pole or electricity pylon you can also create some bizarre-looking compositions. Make sure this doesn't happen by spending just a moment studying your surroundings first.

Keep it Level

If you have a strong horizontal line in your photo, such as the horizon itself, it's crucial to keep it level in the viewfinder. If you don't, your scene will look as if it is slowly rolling downhill and out of the photo! It's very easy to get the horizon, especially if it's the sea, slightly off-level, but you can use the indicators on the viewfinder or on the LCD panel to make sure you're properly aligned.

ABOVE and RIGHT
A subtle slant of the camera may be barely detectable to you but will show up in the printed picture. See how the pagoda, top, is leaning to the left compared to the bottom picture?

FAR LEFT and LEFT
Take care to watch out for surrounding details that may intrude on your picture. On the far left, the tree directly behind Minnie looks as if it's growing out of her head. It is easy to fix the problem by repositioning the people, as shown on the right.

Here Comes the Sun

The sun is essential to many photos. Not only does it light your composition, but bright sunlight also makes colours brighter. Too much sun, directly in the camera lens, however, will cause flare, as pictured below right. Flare is bright patches and circles, often caused by the sunlight reflecting inside the camera lens. Even if the sun is not in the shot, which is something you should avoid, reflections can be a problem. By changing your position slightly, you can often help to remove these unwanted intrusions.

Too Far Away

When you're taking a photo of a group of friends, for example, you want to capture their expressions and mood. We tend to shoot them when they are too far away, as seen in this picture, near right. Moving in close – either physically, or by using a zoom lens – gives a much better result (see far right), especially as average photo prints tend to be fairly small, so it's crucial to make best use of the space.

Check Your Focus

Today, autofocusing mechanisms are fast and accurate, but that's not to say they get it right all the time. With some cameras (such as SLRs and digital cameras with LCD screens) you can check the focus before releasing the shutter. On other cameras you need to ensure that the focus area marked in the viewfinder is exactly over the subject. Take extra care in dim or shadowy conditions, when focus mechanisms often struggle more. The image of the seal, above right, was taken in haste and in an environment of lighting contrasts; with more care you can get the superbly focused shot on the left.

CREATING A BLOCKBUSTER MOVIE

Or at least a mini movie. Digital cameras don't just take still images – most will record movie clips, too. Mobile phones increasingly offer the chance to record short lengths of movie footage, and the quality can be surprisingly good.

Shooting Movies

Taking a movie using your digital camera is simply a matter of selecting the movie mode. This may be an option on the command dial (usually indicated by an old-style movie camera icon) or a switch on the back.

When you switch to movie mode the camera usually changes its resolution. Rather than the millions of pixels recorded for each digital photo, you'll record a smaller number – just 640 x 480 pixels, or sometimes less. This is plenty to display a great movie on your computer or TV. VGA is roughly the same as the quality on a conventional television replaying a VHS videotape. The sound will usually be mono – just a single microphone rather than the two (that give stereo sound) found on movie camcorders.

Most of the camera controls, including the zoom, autofocus and white balance, still work in this mode so you can be sure that your movie subjects will stay in focus throughout and that you can adjust the zoom to get the best view of them.

When you shoot movie clips with a digital camera you will see the time left to record displayed on the LCD panel. This will vary according to the camera model and the memory card space, but space permitting you should be able to shoot any number of movie scenes or clips.

LEFT Whether you are using a digital movie recorder or a still camera that also takes movies, get used to the controls before you start. This will make it easier for you to capture some truly great moments without having to spend time searching for the correct dials.

Viewing Movie Clips

You can watch individual movie clips using QuickTime Player or Windows Media Viewer, but you will only be able to look at individual clips in this way. To compile a movie you will need to join the clips together. Some cameras feature simple editing controls to help you do this; otherwise you'll need to use some software on your computer.

The good news is that this software is remarkably easy to use. Some applications will even do the job automatically, stringing together consecutive clips and adding a musical soundtrack for you. Windows Movie Maker (for PC computers) and iMovie (for Macs) are good applications for creating movies.

MOVIE TIPS

- Keep the camera still. You will get better results if you keep the camera still and let the subjects do the moving.
- Zoom before shooting. Adjust the zoom lens before shooting your movie clips. Zooming during a shot can be uncomfortable for your audience to watch.
- Keep your shots between 7 and 12 seconds. Short scenes don't give viewers a chance to take in the content, while long shots will bore them!
- Hold the camera level. Any tilt of the camera will be very obvious and don't be tempted to turn the camera into portrait mode.

PHOTO THEMES

Someone once said that a great photo was 25 per cent technical knowledge, 25 per cent inspiration and 50 per cent luck. We can't do much about the luck, but having explored how a camera works and some key techniques, let's look at the inspiration. There is no end to the uses you can put your camera to, and taking it with you wherever you go means that you'll never miss out on an opportunity to use it.

In this chapter we'll take a look at some popular photo themes and opportunities, and how to make the best of them.

HOLIDAYS

No matter where you go or what you like doing, there is no doubt that trips away, whether a day out or a long vacation, get us snapping. More photos are taken on a holiday than at any other time, so here are a few guidelines for getting the best from your break.

Tell a Story

We've said this already, but you'll get much better lasting memories of your trip if you tell a story. A holiday is not a series of individual events, it's an adventure. Show your departure (by car, plane or even on foot), then the key events as they happen and finally record your return home. When you get back you'll be able to create an album, a slideshow or even a storyboard that reflects your trip from start to finish.

BELOW Start your photostory with the point of departure, such as boarding a plane (see also pages 54–5).

Fun on the Beach

Beaches are great places for photos in both summer and winter. You can photograph family and friends enjoying the water, building sandcastles or even burying Dad in the sand. You'll get particularly effective results if you shoot from a low angle. Keep your camera clean and dry though (see page 35) or invest in a single-use camera.

Watch out for Shadows

Many holidays take us to bright locations where the sun is high in the sky. This leads to harsh shadows and contrast. Use your camera's fill-in flash to soften the shadows and give your photos more sparkle. If your camera doesn't have a fill-in flash mode, don't worry. Just shoot one photo with the flash on and another without it – you can choose the best shot later. Remember, you can use the flash to give better results if the sun is behind your subjects. When the sun is in the background the people in your photographs won't be squinting in the sunlight, but the shot may be underexposed so a flash is useful.

BELOW The picture below left was taken without fill-in flash while the one on the right used flash to even out the bright backlight.

Shooting Landmarks

If you're going somewhere that is well known for its landmarks, don't forget to take pictures of them! These will give you a 'feel' for the place, and including friends and family will provide even more interest. In really big landscapes, including people also helps to give a sense of scale. And don't forget unusual angles.

In the pictures below the photographer shot the Eiffel Tower in Paris in the evening. She then returned the next day to climb the tower – using the stairs! By photographing downwards from the staircase she could really show how high she had climbed. The tiny people on the ground help to show the sense of scale.

Look for Details

Theme parks are another favourite spot to visit and are full of colourful features. Look out for the information sheets that give details of the day's events. That way you'll know if there are any special performances, shows or events and you'll be in the right place and at the right time to enjoy and photograph them.

Find a Good Location

You'll get better photos by standing in the right place. In some theme parks, zoos and national parks you'll find photo spots already identified. Stand here and you're guaranteed to be in the right place. All you have to do is to make sure you time the shot well, so that the light is right, and that you have something interesting in the foreground to make the shot even better.

When the Sun Goes Down...

... many of us put away our cameras, but don't! Sunsets make great photos, especially in exotic locations. Even as the sun sinks below the horizon you can still grab some terrific photo opportunities. Floodlit buildings, street scenes and even street performers produce terrific results and are great for introducing variety into your photo collection. Remember to prop your camera up so that it doesn't move when taking night shots – in all but the brightest cases your camera will need a long exposure.

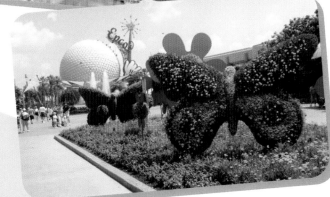

STAY CLEAN AND DRY

Many holiday locations can be hostile for cameras. Sand, dust and water can all damage delicate equipment so you must make sure your camera is protected. You can get special bags that are water- and dust-proof, or just improvise with a plastic bag. If you are still concerned, then go for a single-use camera. You can purchase models that are designed to go in water so you can use them in places you wouldn't dare take any other camera.

LEFT Aquapac bags are widely available in a range of sizes. You can even go diving with some of these, sure in the knowledge that your camera is fully protected.

PERFECT PORTRAITS

Portraits are the next most popular form of photography. Some people automatically think of those staged shots that you can get done at a local photo studio. In fact, portraits are far more varied and include all the sort of informal shots of people that provide lasting memories.

Photographers often say that achieving good portraits is the most difficult thing to do. That may be true with conventional cameras, but digital photography gives us a terrific advantage. We can shoot as many shots as we like and if we don't like the results, we can delete them and shoot some more.

ABOVE A zoom was used in this shot to come in close on the girl's expression and blur the background details so she stands out even more.

ABOVE Group shots work best when you have an uncluttered background. You may find it helpful to focus on the faces in the group and eliminate as much of the setting as you can.

MOVE CLOSER OR ZOOM
Using the zoom lens is an alternative to moving in close. In the case of portraits it is often better to use a zoom lens rather than moving physically closer, as this can make faces look fatter and rounder than they actually are. Zooming in also helps to narrow the depth of field (see pages 18–19) and blur the surroundings.

Framing
Because portraits are photos of people, or people's faces, zooming in close usually gives the best results. Up close you can see the subject's expression and the technique also helps isolate your subject from the surroundings. By going in really close, you can get a more impressive or unusual portrait.

Background
A portrait is a photo of a single person or a group of people. If you have a cluttered background it can distract attention from the subject, which gives a less effective result. If you can't find a plain background, zoom in to blur the background.

Watch the Eyes

The eyes are the most important part of a face so make sure your camera focuses on them and not the end of your subject's nose! It can be difficult to make sure someone in your group shot isn't blinking (as shown left), and when a group gets large, it is almost inevitable that someone will blink. Make sure you take several shots so you stand a reasonable chance of getting at least one with all the eyes open!

Lighting

Soft lighting makes pleasant portraits; harsh lighting causes screwed-up eyes and deep shadows, as below left. Use the camera's flash (see page 33) to fill in any dark shadows and give a softer overall effect.

Anticipation

Some subjects, babies for example, are anything but cooperative! Learn to anticipate how they move and what they do, and then you can be sure to catch them at their cutest, as the photos above show!

Be Creative

Some of the best portraits come from breaking the rules. The wedding portrait, shown below, is blurred, incorrectly lit and hand held, even though the exposures were long, but isn't it wonderful? The photographer just set the camera to automatic, no flash and hoped for the best. By using a digital camera he could see the results straight away. The lesson? If in doubt, just try it.

PHOTOGRAPHING PETS

Animals can be lovable and cuddly or even ferocious and intimidating, but no matter how they look they make great photographs. Here's our guide on capturing the best photo of your pets, or indeed any animals, on film.

Photographing animals is very like photographing people. We can take formal portraits or less formal photos of them doing what they love best – playing with a favourite toy, chasing across the lawn or swimming in and out of fish-tank scenery. The crucial difference is that pets rarely behave or perform on cue like we might expect our friends and family to!

ABOVE Kneel to take a portrait of your pet so you are on a closer level. Remember that you do not always want to use the camera horizontally – turn it vertically if it suits the subject better.

Patience
It's unlikely your pet will perform when you want them to and in the spot you prefer them, so be patient. Have a camera handy so you can grab a shot when he or she is doing something interesting. If you are attempting a portrait, don't expect animals to be as tolerant (or understanding) as human subjects!

Move in Close and Low
Your photos will have more impact if you move in close to your pet (or use the zoom control) so that the pet fills the viewfinder. This also helps to eliminate nearby objects that might prove distracting to anyone looking at the photos later. Get down to the pet's level by kneeling, lying on a carpet or using adjustable viewfinders on digital cameras to get low-level shots.

LEFT Nemo's cousin was photographed by setting the camera to focus on the fish's favourite patch of weed and waiting for him to swim across.

BELOW To ensure that the horse is the subject of this picture, the animal has been centred in the picture frame.

Use Props

If your pet isn't performing as requested, use a prop. A favourite toy (or some food) can help to capture your pet's attention for just long enough to get that perfect shot. You can hold the prop out of sight of the camera or include it to improve the composition in the scene. People can count as props, too – a pet playing with its owner makes for some great photos.

Take Lots of Photos

This is much easier for the digital camera owner, who has no film costs. If you can, take lots of photos, in a sequence, to increase your chances of getting that perfect shot. Remember what we said earlier about professional photographers taking a whole roll of film to achieve just one good image? Perhaps you don't need to go to that extreme, but the more you shoot, the better the opportunity – especially if you pay attention to our final tip below.

Action Please!

It's natural for your pets to move, whether swimming, running, jumping or just playing. So make sure you record them in action. Use a fast film (see page 43) or set your digital camera to high sensitivity. It often helps to pre-set the camera to focus on a particular point and then to shoot when the pet plays there.

BELOW Keeping a distance and using the zoom lens let the photographer capture a natural shot of her dog guarding the car.

HOBBIES AND INTERESTS

If you have a hobby or interest, other than photography of course, chances are that you devote a lot of time and effort to it. So get even more out of it with your camera!

Collections

You might have a collection that's worth recording in some way. Photography can help you to keep track of your collection and to show other collectors what you have. In the case of small items, such as coins or stamps, it can reveal tiny details that are not so easily visible with the naked eye. When photographing objects close up, it's worthwhile supporting your camera either using a mini tripod, as below, or even a pile of books. That way you can check the object is in focus and arrange the lighting accordingly.

ABOVE and RIGHT The closer you can get to the objects, the more detail you'll record and the narrower the depth of field. You may want to shoot a main picture of the entire object as well as lots of close-up detail shots.

Model Making

Modelling presents some interesting photographic opportunities. For example, you could take pictures as your model develops so you have a visual record of all the effort that went into making it. You could be even more creative by digitally editing photos of the finished item so your model plane, for example, really looks as if it is flying through the clouds. Some basic editing techniques are discussed a little later in the book, but here the model plane has been digitally cut out of the original image, using a simple image manipulation programme such as Photoshop Elements, and placed on some landscape photos. A blur filter, selected from the Filters menu of an image manipulation program, will give the impression of motion.

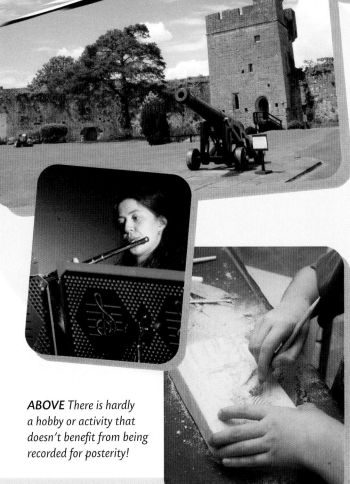

ABOVE There is hardly a hobby or activity that doesn't benefit from being recorded for posterity!

Activities

If you are into sports, gym, ballet or scouting, your camera can come into its own here. Records of sports games, performances or activities are a great way to keep a personal, or even group, journal. Of course, if you are a crucial part of the action you'll need to appoint someone else to do some of the photography.

If you enjoy walking, cycling or travelling, then your opportunities for photography are almost endless. In these cases you will get a better representation of the day or the trip if you shoot the whole event as a photostory, described for holidays on pages 32–3.

SPORTS AND ACTION

Take a look around any sports venue and you'll see professional photographers laden with very expensive equipment attempting to capture every key moment of the game. Even with simple cameras you can take some really impressive action and sports shots. Here are our top tips for getting the best action photographs.

Know Your Game

Football or rugby, diving or climbing, whatever the sport or activity, you have to know it well in order to photograph it successfully. You need to know where on the pitch the action is most likely to take place, the best angles on a rock face or the spot where a parachutist will land. Armed with this kind of knowledge, you'll be able to get frame-filling action.

Take Lots of Photos

Professional sports photographers take a huge number of photographs at a time. They are trying to capture an almost-elusive moment, the split second when the shot is ideally composed, features key action and when the participants are full of emotion. There really is no substitute for knowing your game and then shooting lots of photos. You may throw most of them away, but the few you keep will be stunning!

Shoot Sequences

The cameras that belong to professional photographers have motor drives that can shoot a roll of film in seconds, capturing every part of the action, as in the shots of the dolphin, left. Most amateurs can rarely afford to shoot this much film, but most conventional cameras have a motor drive (or motor drive equivalent in the case of digital cameras) option that lets you take several shots in close succession.

Follow the Action

So far we've talked about how important it is to keep the camera still at all times. In action photography we often need to ensure that the camera moves freely while we follow the action – a person, a racing car or even an aircraft. This will keep our subject sharp but blur the background, which is an essential way to convey a sense of speed and motion.

Use Fast Film or High Sensitivity Setting

Choose a fast film (denoted by an ISO setting of 800 or even 1600), or set your digital camera to a similar rating. With high speeds like this, the shutter speed must be fast in order to capture your subject in motion. You can also catch some extreme expressions in this way. With subjects like the swimmer, shown far right and photographed from below, the fast shutter speed has frozen the water droplets and bubbles.

Get Close

You'll achieve the best shots if you can get in close with your camera. On the field this means making the best of the zoom lens – even so, the action may still seem a long way off. You can fix this later by printing your image larger and trimming it down to just the central area. If you are manipulating your photos digitally on the computer, you can achieve the same effect by electronically cropping the image, as shown in the airplane shot, left.

PARTIES AND CELEBRATIONS

Weddings, birthdays, discos and reunions all provide fantastic photo opportunities. Here's a few tips to help you take some great pictures.

ABOVE Taking group shots is a challenge, especially informal shots, such as at a wedding or ceremony. If the group is looking too posed and artificial, try changing the setting; an outdoor setting can add colour and natural light that results in a better photo.

Stay Alert!

The first tip is about ensuring that you keep your camera safe and away from the food and drinks! It's easy at a party to get carried away and to end up splashing your valuable hardware with sticky food or drinks. Using a waterproof housing may be a step too far, but if you know you could be in for a messy time a single use camera might be a good bet!

Atmosphere

Night parties and discos can be dark, so using a flash is pretty essential. Unfortunately, a bright flash can ruin the atmosphere in your photos, so one way to keep at least some of the action, if your camera will allow it, is to set a longer shutter speed than is normal. At between $\frac{1}{8}$ and $\frac{1}{15}$ of a second you'll get the key subjects illuminated by the flash and also, while the shutter remains open, you'll have the movement and action on the dance floor!

Red Eye

When it's dark our eyes compensate by opening up the iris to let in as much light as possible. This is great for helping us to see in the dark, but photographically it's a nightmare! When you shoot people with a flash under these conditions, red eye can be a problem. It happens when the light from the flash reflects off the back of the subject's eyes, illuminating the fine red blood vessels (dogs and cats suffer from green-eye!). You can work around this by getting people to look sideways or by selecting the red-eye flash mode to reduce (but often not eliminate) the effect. This uses a series of pre-flashes to reduce the subject's iris size before taking the picture, but you can also correct it later. You can digitally remove red eye on a computer (see page 59) and if you've already got prints, special red-eye pens (available from most photo stores) will invisibly return irises to black.

Don't Shoot the Groups, Shoot the Action

Family celebration photos can be really dull! They may end up as a series of stiff, obviously posed photos of camera-shy relatives who look awkward and uncomfortable with false smiles. Grandma might expect you to take these kinds of pictures, but make sure you take some action shots too. People dancing, the birthday boy or girl blowing out the candles on the cake, people laughing or singing – all of these will make far better and more memorable photos of the event. You will also catch people in their more natural state and they will soon forget to feel awkward in front of the lens.

REMEMBER THE DETAILS
Parties and celebrations are people centred events, but it's also important not to forget the other features – the birthday cake or decorations, for example. Details like this help us to create, and in later years to remember, the whole event.

LEFT and ABOVE Timing is everything so don't be afraid to shoot multiples. Catching the candles being blown out leads to an even better picture a second or two later.

WHAT HAPPENS NEXT?

You've taken your photos, so what happens now? Well, that all depends on the type of camera you've used and what you want to do with the results. Let's first take a look at what happens once you've taken your photos and returned from a great day out.

WHERE DO YOUR PHOTOS COME FROM?

Film Camera

With a conventional film camera you'll end up with your treasured shots on a roll, or perhaps several rolls, of film. Not so long ago many people processed their films (to produce slides or negatives from which prints could be made) at home. These days, commercial processing at your local photo store or by mail order is very quick, cheap and (perhaps most importantly) reliable! And you don't have to expose yourself to any chemicals.

When you take, or send, your films to a lab your precious memories are loaded into a minilab – a totally automated processing centre. The film goes in one end and is processed to produce negatives or slides that are dried and finally printed. There is no need for a darkroom and the process takes between 30 and 60 minutes. If you want to edit and play with your photos on a computer you can even have a picture disc, containing digital copies of your images, produced at the same time.

Digital Camera

If you've got a digital camera, your images will be safely recorded on digital film – memory cards. With these you have a choice:

• Load the images directly from your camera to your computer.
• Take the memory card to a photolab, just like film.
• Take the memory card to a kiosk and create prints yourself (see the procedure opposite).

Whether you choose to load images on to your computer or to take them directly to a photolab, it's a good idea to put the images from the memory card on to a CD. This means that you will have a permanent copy of the originals so that you can wipe your memory cards clean and use them again.

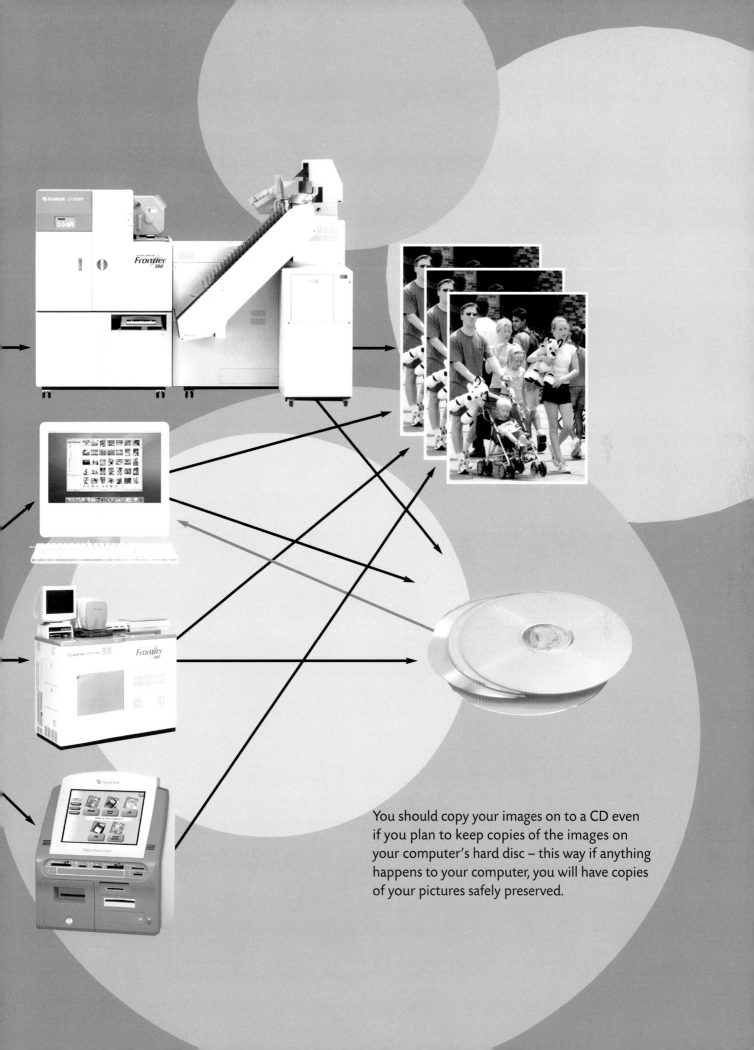

You should copy your images on to a CD even if you plan to keep copies of the images on your computer's hard disc – this way if anything happens to your computer, you will have copies of your pictures safely preserved.

Printing from Camera Phones

If you have a camera phone, it's great to be able to send or e-mail photos to friends' computers or phones. In order to preserve your photo adventures, however, you will also want to print them out.

You can print from a computer by e-mailing the photos from your phone to your computer, and then by treating the images in exactly the same way as you would if you had downloaded them from a CD or a memory card. Kodak, and other companies, offer a printing service where you can e-mail your photos from your phone directly to their labs. As if by magic, just a few days later the prints will drop through your letterbox.

Direct printers are, perhaps, the most fun way to get prints from your phone. If your camera phone has an infrared or Bluetooth feature, you can beam your photos directly to special printers that accommodate this facility – like the one pictured below. The great thing about these printers is how portable they are. Although they may not fit the smallest of pockets, you can carry them around with you and they are great for sharing party photos with your friends!

Photo Kiosks

Many camera stores and photolabs now feature kiosks like the one pictured above. These are small computer-based units that let you create your own prints from images on a memory card or from a CD. You simply stick your memory card or CD into the machine and up comes a preview of all the images on the kiosk's screen. Next, you choose which ones you want to print, what size you want and the number of copies. You can even trim the images (to print only part of the photo), correct errors (such as red eye) or use special effects.

PHOTO BONANZA

Whether you choose a local photolab or an online photo store, you will find that most of these printing services offer much more than just straightforward prints. You may have your photo masterpieces applied to almost anything – mugs, T-shirts, jigsaws, mousemats and more. These products can make great gifts for family and friends, with a very personal touch.

Online services will even produce hardback, professionally bound albums of your photo collections, as shown below. You can choose how your prints are displayed and add captions and colours, all on your computer. Send off the results by e-mail and, days later, your album will be delivered to your door. You may select themes and layouts too, so forget those old-fashioned, sombre volumes of family photos – these are albums for the twenty-first century!

Florida 2004

7

PRINTING AT HOME

With a digital camera, not only can you review and enjoy your photos on a computer, but you can also produce paper prints at home with a printer. If you use special photo paper, which gives glossy, matt or satin finishes, the photographs will not deteriorate significantly over the years and the paper is also designed to match the inks used by your printer to deliver the sharpest results – even the printer you use with your computer will be able to give you some fantastic prints for you to share or put in an album. Let's take a look at what's on offer.

Look, No Computer!

Some printers are designed to give you great prints, directly from your camera – just like the ones you get from a photo lab. These printers are compact and some are even battery operated so you can use them anywhere.

Most of these printers use a process called dye sublimation to produce high quality, glossy prints that can stand pretty rough handling. The colours are produced by evaporating coloured dyes and transferring them to a print – this delivers vibrant, longlasting colours. These printers can be rather costly to run, as the paper and ink is expensive, and you can only produce small prints. But you don't have to use a computer – you can produce your prints quickly and easily and some models don't even need a cable to connect – the camera and printer can talk wirelessly!

ABOVE RIGHT Printers like this Canon model can produce prints direct from the camera, through a simple connection.

BELOW This all-in-one printer features memory card slots (just above the paper tray) for direct photo printing.

All-in-One Printers

Some computer printers don't just let you print boring black-and-white documents. All-in-one printers also make copies of pictures (just like a photocopier), send faxes down the telephone line, print colour documents and even print photos directly.

Apart from printing conventionally through the computer, you may also be able to connect your camera directly to the printer, just like the printers described opposite. You can even slot the camera's memory card directly into some printers. These printers often have several memory card slots, so if you have one sort of memory card in your digital camera and another in your camera phone, no problem, you can print from both!

Because you can't see what's on the memory card you can print a sheet of paper that shows all the photos as small thumbnails. You can then choose which ones to print at full size without wasting paper. Some printers even have a small LCD screen to let you preview the images.

Inkjet Printers

If you want to edit your photographs on your computer before you print them (see pages 58–61 for photo-editing information and techniques), then you can use a standard inkjet printer. Most of today's inkjet printers offer photo-quality results and larger versions can even produce impressive large-scale prints.

LEFT If you want to edit your photos on a computer, an inkjet printer is great for printing out the results.

IDEAS AND INSPIRATIONS

Taking photos and sharing them is a great activity in itself, but you can have even more fun using your photos as part of a project. Here are just a few ideas for projects to do using your photos.

SHARING YOUR PICTURES

Create a CD or DVD Slideshow

If you've got a large and growing collection of digital images, it makes sense to keep a backup on CD or DVD. As well as making simple backups, it's also very easy to make slideshows of your pictures to enjoy on your computer or DVD player.

To start with, you'll need computer software, such as Roxio's MyDVD and Slideshow or Ulead's CD and DVD PictureShow. Follow the instructions and you'll be amazed at just how easy it is to make a professional-looking slideshow, complete with music and clever transitions between slides and even menus.

BELOW *Ulead's CD and DVD PictureShow makes it simple to create bold titles and menus and then add photos to each of the menu items.*

LEFT *Roxio's MyDVD and Slideshow lets you combine photos with movies, and even recordings made from TV shows!*

Web Photo Galleries

You share your photos with friends and family, so why not share them with the world? Creating a web photo gallery that can be seen by anyone on the Internet is not as difficult as it sounds.

The easiest way to start is to sign up to an online service that lets you store and share your images. You can upload images to display in the gallery and allow visitors to review them. Some services even let visitors order prints from your selected photos. This is an ideal way to share photos with distant friends or relatives, who can then put them into their albums. Take a look at Shutterfly (www.shutterfly.com) or the Kodak share site (www.kodakgallery.com).

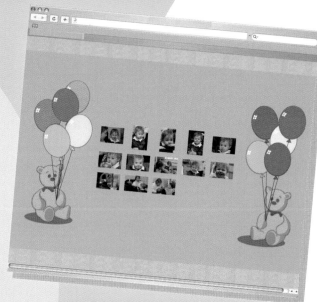

If you are feeling a little more ambitious, image-editing software often includes features for creating web-based galleries. In Photoshop Elements, a popular application for many digital photographers, you can build elaborate galleries with comparative ease. Templates, like the teddy bears seen here, make it simple to create a website with a theme.

MAKE YOUR iPOD PERSONAL

You fill your iPod with your personal music collection, so why not make it look special to you too? Thanks to Hewlett-Packard's Custom Tattoo, you can use one of your own photos to make a covering for your iPod. If you are lucky enough to own an iPod Photo, you can carry your photo collection around in your pocket. You can review images on the small screen or attach it to a TV for your friends and family to share.

PHOTOSTORIES AND COLLAGES

If you've been carefully taking photos so they tell a story, why not make them into a collage or photostory? This is a great basis for a page in a scrapbook or, if you've got enough images, a poster.

The idea behind a photostory is, obviously, to tell a story through photos alone. To do this you need to have a series of photos that clearly show a sequence. Here are a few ideas, along with the photos, for telling a story.

• *A Day Out:* Photos of the journey, your destination and the journey home. Include some title shots, such as the gates of the theme park or zoo, along with some detail pictures of your friends or family watching events, eating lunch and generally having fun.

• *A Special Day:* Weddings, christenings and other social events. Take photos of the main events, guests arriving, people playing around and some general shots of the venues. Close-ups of people watching the event come in useful for linking parts of the story together.

• *Best Friend:* Photos of a good friend or family member taken over a couple of years or more. Include milestones such as first day at school, birthdays and holidays.

• *Favourite Place:* Photos taken at different times of the day, from different locations. Concentrate on the details as well as overall shots and people enjoying their visit.

Now it's time to have fun. Move the images around so they tell a story. Your eyes should flow easily from one shot to another. Keep rearranging until you get the effect that looks the best. To make it even more visually interesting, consider tilting, overlapping or trimming the photos into unusual shapes that work with the sequence.

PHOTOSTORY TIPS

• There is no right and wrong way to create photostories or collages. If it looks good to you, then it probably is good!

• Don't be afraid to experiment. You don't have to use rectangular prints and regular arrangements.

• If it helps with the storyline, add arrows to lead viewers from one image to another.

• You don't have to actually take the photos in order, or even at the same time. If you forget to take a shot of leaving the house in the morning, fake it on your return or shoot it the next day!

To assemble your photos, begin by laying them out so you can get an overall view of them all and how they might work together. If you are working with prints, do this on a large flat surface, such as a table, as seen left. If you're using digital photos, copy them all on to the computer's desktop.

The photostory on the opposite page is a story of a girl's trip to see a Concorde plane. The ticket has been used as a 'start' photo and a title shot as the 'end' photo. Within the story we get to tour around the outside and inside of the aircraft. Though it doesn't always need it, you can caption your photos, too. You can do this by using sticky notes or, if you're creating the collage on your computer, by adding text panels. For this digital composition, notes have been added and the prints have been given white borders to make them stand out more.

My boarding pass for Concorde

Here we are!

My brother and I prepare to board

The windows are really tiny

Me at twice the speed of sound

Look at the controls

I'm only just taller than the wheels

A Great Day! I wish I could have flown it

MAKE YOUR OWN GREETINGS CARDS

Perhaps the best way to show off your photo skills is to create your own greetings cards. They're ideal for sending to friends and family, for special occasions or just to say hello or thanks!

Handmade Cards

You can get kits from most craft and stationery stores that let you mount your photographs in windowed cards and then apply embellishments. This is ideal for personalizing the cards or making them especially appropriate to a particular event.

If you are more ambitious you can start from scratch by using decorative card stock, which is available in a wide range of sizes, designs and colours. Be adventurous – there is no right or wrong way to make a greetings card and you only have to please yourself.

Fold a rectangular piece of card in half widthways and cut a hole in the front. You might like to cut out a pumpkin silhouette for a Halloween card or perhaps a heart for Valentine's Day. Simple, bold designs work best.

Stick your photo to the inside of the card so only the central area is visible through the hole – when you open the card the entire photo will be revealed. Remember to leave enough space for your personal message on the inside front cover. To make the card extra special you could also buy some embossed lettering to enhance the front cover. Messages like 'Happy Birthday', 'Christmas Greetings' or 'Best Wishes' are easily obtained and transfer lettering can be used to make up individual messages.

ABOVE and LEFT
Frames like these are widely available from craft stores and as downloads from the Internet. You can mount your photo in the centre or cut the central area out to reveal a photo inside.

Digital Greetings

If you have a computer, you can print your own cards. In fact, some photo-editing software contains special sections just for this. They will let you combine a photo with words and graphics, such as cartoon characters, toys or animals, to produce a professional looking card that you can print using your computer's printer.

Again, if you are more ambitious, you can create your own, very individual card by doing all the work yourself. You can buy clip art images on CDs or download them from the Internet; these can then be combined with your own photos and words to make a truly unique card.

Use the Text tool in your image-editing software to add a title or phrase and apply special effects to the text, such as shadows or glows. Even simple text effects like coloured lettering can make a lot of impact. When you are finished you can print the results or even e-mail the greeting directly to your friends!

CHEAT
If you want an easy way to produce greetings cards, visit your online photolab or photo store. Choose your frame, words and layout and let them make it for you! The downside is that it's not quite as personal and it will cost more than creating your own cards!

ABOVE and LEFT
Here the Text tool in the image-editing software was used to add a title to the picture – essential for providing information that the recipient of the card may not know.

PHOTO-EDITING ON YOUR COMPUTER

Photo-editing software, sometimes called image-manipulation software, is a great way to improve photos that aren't quite perfect. It is also ideal for creating special effects or 'art effect' pictures from your photos. Here's just a taste of what you can do with a few mouse clicks. The techniques are easy to learn, but can give impressive results.

Brightness and Contrast

Sometimes, because of poor weather or bad lighting, our photos can come out a little dull. There's a simple solution to this – the Brightness/Contrast feature, which is common to all types of software. When you select this, you'll see a dialogue box appear with two sliders – one for brightness and one for contrast. Slide to the right and you'll increase the brightness or contrast; slide to the left and you'll reduce them. Try it out by moving the sliders to the left and right in different combinations. Some programs have a feature called Auto Enhance, Auto Fix or Auto Levels. Click on this and the brightness, contrast and colour will be adjusted automatically.

BELOW The Brightness/Contrast feature was used to convert the dull top picture to the more vibrant one below.

ABOVE The Saturation tool was used to add colour, especially evident in the sky and playground equipment.

More Colour

Sometimes our photos don't just look duller, they also appear less colourful – the bright blue skies and vivid landscapes seem less vibrant. Often this is because the camera records the actual scene rather than our memories, which can be enhanced by a happy mood. Even so, all software makes it is simple to make the scene look brighter using the Saturation tool. Often this is combined with the hue control. To increase the amount of colour (the saturation) move the slider to the right. Don't overdo it though, about ten percent should be enough – any more will produce lurid and unrealistic colour!

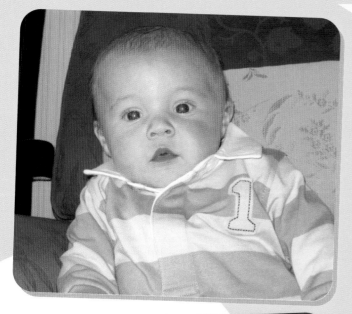

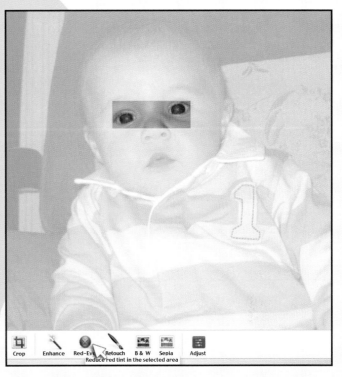

ABOVE, CLOCKWISE The original photograph of the baby shows him with unfortunate red eye. The digital image is manipulated by using the Red Eye tool to select both eyes. The finished picture appears with the red eye removed.

Correcting Red Eye

Red eye is caused when the flash from your camera reflects off the back of a subject's eye. All the blood vessels are illuminated and the result can be pretty scary! Use the Red Eye tool to select the eyes, either individually or together. Click the OK button to correct the red eye and instantly your subjects will have a normal expression again!

PHOTO-EDITING SOFTWARE

There's a lot of this available! If you don't already have it, here are some names to look out for – most work with Macs and PCs. Check the software that came with your digital camera too, as you'll usually find some software included.

- Adobe Photoshop Elements: A user-friendly version of Adobe Photoshop, which is used by professional designers.
- ArcSoft PhotoStudio/Photo Impression: This is a great product and is often supplied with digital cameras.
- Ulead PhotoImpact: Easy to use and comprehensive.
- Jasc Paint Shop Pro: Perhaps a little too complicated for newcomers, but great for the enthusiast.
- Roxio Photosuite: The best application if you enjoy using photos to make greetings cards, posters and albums.

A New Sky

If you've got some great photos of friends or your family, but the photos are spoiled by a dull overcast sky, don't worry. You can make the photo really impressive by adding a new, spectacular sky.

Pictured on the left is an example of how a great photo can be let down by other elements in the picture, which sometimes may be out of your control, or aren't actually noticeable until after you see the picture on-screen or printed out. Although the top picture is charming, it has a very grey sky, but if you have another photo of a much more interesting sky, you can combine the two.

To do this, start by selecting a tool called the Magic Wand – it may have another name in your software package, but it is most often called this. Using the Magic Wand, select the parts of a photo that are the same colour – in this case select the sky in the original photo. Sometimes you have to click on a few regions of the sky to make sure that it is all selected. Once selected, you will see a dotted line around the edge of the sky.

Open the second image, containing the attractive skyscape. You will need to select all of this so that you can paste it into the first image. Try using the keyboard shortcut of Control Key + A (Command + A on a Mac) to select the entire image. Then Control + C (Command + C on a Mac) to copy the image on to the computer's clipboard. The clipboard temporarily stores copied images so that they can be pasted elsewhere.

Now, return to the original image. Normally, when you copy from one image to another you use the Paste command (in the Edit menu), but to paste the new sky into the area selected with the Magic Wand, use Paste Into. And, hey presto, new sky!

LEFT The grey sky in the top picture has been replaced with the blue sky from a second picture using the Magic Wand feature. The final combined result appears at the bottom.

ABOVE *Here you see how cloned pixels of grass and shrubs are used to fill in, bit by bit, the areas you wish to remove.*

Cloning

The great thing about photo manipulation is that, not only can you copy one image into another, as we did with the sky, but we can also move selected parts of the same image to hide objects or to reposition them. This process is called cloning because we are copying pixels (the little coloured squares that make up the image) from one place to another. This technique is used here to clean up the background of the photo of a band member.

To clone an image, first choose the pixels that you want to repeat using the Clone facility on your software. In this case, the foreground grass from the left-hand side is selected and cloned on to the right, to cover the people and objects on the grass that clutter the background. You can now use different parts of the background to remove (cover up) any other distractions – here, part of the shrubbery was used to fill in and simplify the background scenery.

RIGHT The background people have been covered up by cloned grass and trees to create an impressive portrait of a musician.

MANIPULATING HELP
Here's a useful tip. Most photo-editing software includes help, tips or tutorials that will guide you, step by step, through manipulations like this and much more.

JARGON BUSTER

Analogue In photography this is a term applied to conventional, non-digital cameras and processes.

Aperture The size of the opening in a camera's lens. A larger aperture allows more light to reach the film or electronic sensor in a digital camera.

Autofocus A system found in most cameras that automatically focuses the lens on the subject. Indicators in the viewfinder ensure that the camera focuses on the spot that the photographer chooses.

Automatic Exposure A camera mode sometimes marked Auto or AE, in which the camera automatically sets the controls for a perfect exposure.

Backlight Compensation A setting that is found on some cameras, or one that can be set manually, that increases the exposure to prevent subjects lit from behind being overexposed.

Burst Mode Feature on a digital camera that enables a series of photos to be taken at short intervals. Motor drives in conventional cameras do the same thing. Great for action photography.

Card Reader Computer attachment that allows the memory cards from a digital camera to be downloaded. It saves connecting the camera directly up to a computer and using up valuable battery power.

CCD Sensor The light-sensitive part of most digital cameras. The equivalent to film in a conventional camera, the CCD is made up of tightly packed light sensitive transistors, each of which records a part of the image. In the final photo these are represented by the individual picture elements called pixels.

CMOS Sensor An alternative to a CCD sensor. Used in some cameras as it uses less battery power.

Colour Balance The relative amounts of red, green and blue in a photo. When these are the same as in the original scene, the photo has perfect colour balance.

CompactFlash A common form of memory card used in digital cameras.

Composition The arrangement of objects in a photo. For arty effects, photographers place objects carefully in a photo, often making sure that there are no strong lines in the centre or that they are placed too close to the centre.

Compression Because digital photos need a lot of memory to record them, they are often compressed in size to allow more to be recorded on a memory card. Extreme compression causes quality losses in the photo.

Conventional Camera A term used to describe a non-digital camera.

Depth of Field The distance between nearest and farthest points in an image in sharp focus. Narrow depth of field means objects in front of and behind the subject are blurred. Wide depth of field means distant and close objects will be in focus.

Digital Camera A camera that records images as digital data, which can be read by a computer.

Digital Image The photo produced by a digital camera. It is stored in the form of a digital data file.

Digitized Image Photos taken on film can be converted into a digital image by using a scanner. This converts the image into one similar to that taken with a digital camera.

Electronic Flash A flash unit that is built into a camera, or available as an external optional accessory. It provides additional light when the daylight (or other lighting) light levels are low.

Exposure The amount of light that is allowed to reach a camera's sensor or film. The aperture and shutter speed can be changed to make sure the exposure is correct.

f-stop A ratio (of a lens' focal length to diameter) used to describe the aperture of a lens. It is often marked on lenses.

Filter (1) Coloured or distorted glass or plastic that is placed over a camera lens to correct colour balances for special effects.

Filter (2) Part of an image-editing software program that allows effects to be applied to a digital image.

Image Editing Software Computer software that is designed to display digital (or digitized images) and allows them to be manipulated. Manipulations could be corrections (to colour or focus), trimming or more comprehensive changes, such as adding new skies or cloning.

J-PEG Popular file format for storing images on digital cameras. It compresses photo files and therefore allows a large number of images to be stored on a memory card.

Megapixel A short way of saying 'million pixels'. The more pixels there are in an image, the sharper and more detailed it will be.

Memory Card A small memory storage card that can be inserted in a digital camera to store images. Additional cards can be used to allow more shots to be taken before downloading to a computer and reusing the card.

Monopod See unipod.

Panorama/Panoramic Mode A sequence of shots, usually taken around the horizon that can be digitally linked into a single ultra-wide photograph. Conventional cameras use very wide film formats to record panoramas in a single shot.

Photo Printer A printer that produces photographic prints, but often used specifically for computer printers (or those that attach to cameras directly) that are designed to produce photo-quality prints.

Pixel The smallest element of a digital image, which corresponds to a single transistor on the image sensor.

Portrait (1) A photo taken with the camera held vertically.

Portrait (2) Photograph of a person, pet or other object that concentrates on the subject.

Red Eye The reflection of a camera's flash from the back of a subject's eyes. It gives the eyes a bright red appearance and occurs in both conventional and digital cameras.

Resolution The amount of detail in an image. The more pixels in a photo, the higher the resolution and the more detail. Resolution is often described in terms of megapixels (a four-megapixel camera has twice the resolution of a two-megapixel model).

Saturation The amount of colour in a photo; for example, a black-and-white photo is known as unsaturated. In bright sunlight, colours become highly saturated. Saturation can be increased using image-editing software.

Scanner A computer device that allows photos, illustrations or artwork to be 'read' by a computer through a process called 'analogue to digital conversion' or digitizing.

Shutter Release The button that, when pressed, actually takes the photo. In most cases when you half-press this button you will activate the autofocus and exposure system. This means that when you fully press the shutter release, the camera will be perfectly set for your photo.

Shutter Speed The time that a camera's sensor or film is exposed to light during an exposure. Short exposures let in less light and also help to 'freeze' fast action.

Single-use Camera Camera that comes pre-loaded with film and is designed to be used only once. When all shots are taken, the camera is returned to the photolab for processing.

SLR Single Lens Reflex camera: A camera with a special optical system that lets users see the scene that will be recorded on film or digitally through the viewfinder. An optical system of prisms and mirrors allows the image from the lens to be passed on to the viewfinder.

Tripod A three-legged camera support, essential for preventing or limiting camera shake.

Unipod A single-legged camera support. Not as stable as a tripod, but much more compact and lightweight. It is also called a monopod.

Viewfinder An optical system that allows you to see the same part of a scene that the camera records. The view through the viewfinder will change if a zoom lens is used.

White Balance A control found in still and movie digital cameras that changes the colour balance of an image to compensate for colour casts in the scene or lighting. This can be operated automatically, or be manually set.

Zoom Lens A lens with a variable focal length that allows a scene to be enlarged or reduced in scale.

INDEX

PICTURE CREDITS

All photos by Peter Cope, © Carlton Books Limited, except for the following. The publishers would like to thank the sources below for their kind permission to reproduce the pictures in the book.

1. Alamy; 3. Getty Images/Taxi; 7. Alamy; 10. Getty Images/Taxi; 12. Getty Images/Stone; 13. Getty Images/ National Geographic; 14. Getty Images/Taxi; 30. Getty Images/Taxi; 32. Getty Images/Taxi; 36l. Photonica/Bob Elsdale; 36r. Getty Images/Stone; 38t. Alamy; 40r. Getty Images/Stone+; 44. Getty Images/Taxi

Every effort has been made to acknowledge correctly and contact the source and /or copyright holder of each picture, and Carlton Books apologises for any unintentional errors or omissions, which will be corrected in future editions of this book.

AUTHOR'S ACKNOWLEDGEMENTS

Thanks to my children, David and Sarah, for helping with many of the photos in this book. They insisted that we visit Florida to get the best possible pictures! Thanks too to their friends, including Maria, Charlotte, Thomas and Yasmin, who also helped take some great photos.